WHAT IT MEANS TO BE
SERIES

PUBLISHER	Joseph R. DeVarennes
PUBLICATION DIRECTOR	Kenneth H. Pearson
ADVISORS	Roger Aubin
	Robert Furlonger
EDITORIAL MANAGER	Jocelyn Smyth
EDITORS	Ann Martin
	Shelley McGuinness
	Robin Rivers
	Mayta Tannenbaum
ARTISTS	Summer Morse
	Barbara Pileggi
	Steve Pileggi
	Mike Stearns
PRODUCTION MANAGER	Ernest Homewood
PRODUCTION ASSISTANTS	Catherine Gordon
	Kathy Kishimoto
PUBLICATION ADMINISTRATOR	Anna Good

Canadian Cataloguing in Publication Data

Langdon, Anne
    What it means to be—polite

(What it means to be; 5)
ISBN 0-7172-2232-2

1. Courtesy — Juvenile literature.
2. Etiquette — Moral and ethical aspects — Juvenile literature.
I. Pileggi, Steve.   II. Title.   III. Title: Polite.   IV. Series.

BJ1533.C9L36 1987   j177'.1   C87-095049-5

WHAT IT MEANS TO BE...

POLITE

Written by
Anne Langdon

Illustrated by
Steve Pileggi

Being polite is easy when you consider how others feel.

It was a wet, gray afternoon. Kim was in bed with a cold. She was tired of reading and didn't feel like drawing.

Just as she was beginning to feel bored, her mother appeared at her bedroom door. "You have company. Hannah is here to cheer you up!"

"I'm going to do a puppet show for you," Hannah said as she walked into the room. "I made the puppets from my dad's old socks. My mom sewed on buttons for eyes."

Hannah sat on the floor at the foot of Kim's bed. Up came her two hands, each with a puppet. She was so excited she forgot some of the words, and her head and arms showed more than they were supposed to.

Kim had seen better puppet shows, but she didn't tell Hannah that. Instead she said, "Thanks for coming over. You made me feel much better."

It's polite to thank people when they try to help you or make you feel better.

"Please" and "thank you" are polite and helpful words.

Tammy and Andrea were walking home from Kids' Klub on a windy afternoon. They had just finished making colorful kites. As they skipped along the sidewalk, their kites bobbed brightly behind them. It didn't take Paul long to notice them.

"Hey, that looks like fun. Give it to me," he said to Tammy and tried to grab her kite.

"No! It's mine, I made it myself!" she protested.

Andrea, who was a little older, knew the best way to ask for things. "Paul, Tammy might let you have a turn if you asked her nicely," she pointed out.

Paul had to think about it for a minute.

"Tammy, could I please have a turn?" he asked.

"I guess so, but don't take it too far away," she answered.

When it looked as if he might do just that, she called after him, "Don't run off with it, please!"

Paul slowed down and turned to say, "I won't. I'll come right back."

While Paul was running with her kite, Tammy was able to see how beautiful it looked, high up in the blue sky. "That's the best kite I've ever made," she said proudly to Andrea.

"That's the *only* kite you've ever made," Andrea replied with a smile. They both laughed.

As Paul came galloping back to return her kite, Tammy turned to Andrea. "*Thank you* for helping. I'm glad Paul had a turn with my kite."

"Thank you for letting me borrow your kite," said Paul. "It's the first time I've seen a whale that could fly."

People feel better about doing something when they're asked nicely. Saying "please" and "thank you" are the best ways to let others know you appreciate them.

Polite people don't interrupt others when they're talking.

Kim and Paul were chasing each other on the way home from school. They were laughing and running as fast as they could. Soon they were joined by Colette and Bobby who were zooming around pretending they were jet airplanes.

"My mom's going to take me on a plane!" Bobby exclaimed once they got tired and slowed down. "She goes on them all the time, and knows what to do. And—"

"Wow, a plane ride!" Kim cried, interrupting Bobby who hadn't finished talking. "You're lucky! Did you know that . . . ?"

A little later, Colette started telling her friends what had happened to her the day before. "I learned to play 'Twinkle, Twinkle, Little Star' on my accordion. I practiced and practiced and yesterday, I did it! My mom said that I—"

"My mom let me have dinner in the TV room last night," piped in Kim, "because she was going out and the babysitter was coming over!"

Colette sighed. She wanted to tell her friends all about learning a new song, but Kim wouldn't let her finish talking. She felt a bit angry.

Then Paul said, "My birthday is in eight days! I'm going to invite my friends over for a party! It's going to be great. We'll play lots of party games and then—"

"Party games?" Kim burst in, and started jumping up and down. "Do you know the one . . . ?"

Colette, Bobby and Paul looked at each other. Kim was so excited that she kept forgetting to listen to them.

"Kim," said Paul crossly, "you're not the queen of the world!" Kim was suddenly very quiet. She didn't understand why Paul was so upset.

"How come you're mad at me?" she asked.

"Because you never let us finish what we're saying," Bobby replied.

"And that's not fair," Colette added.

"But I had things to tell you," Kim wailed.

"So did we!" said Paul.

"We need to take turns so everyone gets a chance to talk," Colette said finally.

"Tell you what, Kim," Paul suggested with a grin, "when you come to my birthday party, we'll have a special talking game just for you!" Kim thought this was funny. Soon they were all laughing.

You expect people to listen when you have something to say, so you should be willing to listen when they are talking. Talking is one way you can share yourself with others. Listening is a way of letting your friends know you're interested in them.

If you need to talk while others are speaking, say "excuse me" first.

A princess and a punk rocker sitting together? It must be Hallowe'en! Janice and Jason were sitting on the stairs waiting to go out to trick-or-treat. They had spent hours planning and making their costumes. It had been hard work, but now they were ready.

Their mother was going to take them to all the homes in the neighborhood, but right now she was talking to their father. Janice and Jason waited and waited.

Finally Jason pointed to the front window. "Excuse me, Mom and Dad," he said, "but I think I see a clown, a robot and a pirate coming up the path to our door!" Some of the other children had already begun trick-or-treating.

"I guess we should get going too," their mother said smiling. "We don't want to be the last ones out!"

If you have to interrupt someone to say something important, say "excuse me" before you begin talking.

It's polite to make guests feel at home.

Ryan let Hoppy and Blinky out of their cage so they could run around in the backyard. The rabbits wiggled their pink noses in the sunshine and nibbled the grass and dandelions.

Joey came by to visit. "All right! Rabbits. You're so lucky your parents let you have them!"

"Would you like to hold one?" Ryan asked.

"Would I ever!" Joey answered.

While his guest was playing with Blinky, Ryan asked Joey if he wanted some apple juice.

"Yes, please," Joey replied.

"I'll see if Dad will let us have some raisins too. Do you like raisins?"

"I *love* them!" Joey answered, and wiggled his nose at Hoppy.

Before long, Ryan came back carrying two glasses. Behind him was his father, who had a tray of goodies.

"My dad says we can have a picnic!" Ryan exclaimed as he set the glasses down on the picnic table.

"But what about Hoppy and Blinky?" Joey cried. "They don't have any snacks."

"That's what you think," said Ryan with a grin, and he pulled a handful of celery and carrot sticks from his back pocket.

When friends visit you, you should do what you can to make them feel relaxed and happy.

Saying "hello" and "goodbye" to your host or hostess is a polite thing to do.

Paul's grandmother was happy because she had sold a house. Her job was to sell houses. To celebrate, she arrived at Paul's house carrying a big, warm bag of Chinese food! It smelled wonderful.

"Would you like to invite a friend for dinner?" she asked Paul.

"Yes, please. I'll see if Bobby can come," said Paul as he hurried to the phone.

When Bobby arrived, he made sure to say hello to Paul's parents and his grandmother before he sat down to eat. Dinner was fun. There were all sorts of yummy things in cardboard containers with red dragons on them! They even had fortune cookies.

Before leaving, Bobby said goodbye to Paul's parents, and he thanked Paul's grandmother for dinner.

"It was a pleasure having you, Bobby," she said.

Saying "hello" and "goodbye" to your friends and their parents is one way of showing them that you like to vist. They will remember you as being a polite, thoughtful guest.

It's not polite to point, stare or talk about others.

Tammy and Colette's parents had just bought a new car! It was a station wagon with a seat facing the back window. The girls had never seen a seat like that before in a car. It was great!

After dinner their father said, ''Let's go for a ride.'' He was excited too.

The girls sat in the backward seat. Tammy started pointing at people. Colette explained that it wasn't a polite thing to do. It made others feel uncomfortable. They waved to everyone they saw instead. Some friendly people even waved back.

As a special treat, they stopped off at the Donut Delight for dessert on their way home. The elderly lady who served them at the counter was very nice. Tammy asked for a chocolate donut and a grape juice. As they were waiting for the lady to get their order ready, Tammy said to her mother, ''Boy, is she ever *old*!''

Colette gave Tammy a poke and frowned at her. Tammy didn't know why. When they sat down at their table, her mother explained. "It's fine to notice things about other people but it's best to keep your comments to yourself. There's no need to say anything out loud."

"But what if it's something nice?" Tammy asked.

"If you want to compliment someone, tell them directly," her mother replied. "Don't talk about them—it makes them feel they are being stared at, and that makes them uncomfortable."

"There's something I'm staring at," her father said with a laugh, "it's this tray full of donuts and juice. Let's eat!"

No one likes to be singled out. If you notice something different about somebody, it's best not to say anything.

It's polite to give your seat to someone who is elderly, handicapped or having trouble standing.

Mitchell and his mother were riding on a crowded bus. They had just bought a pair of red running shoes for Mitchell.

"I can hardly wait to try them out!" he said. "I bet I'll run faster when I'm wearing them."

"That's right," his mother agreed, "you're getting bigger and faster every day."

"But I'm still only four," he said with a sigh. Just then, the bus stopped to let on an old man with a cane. It looked as if it was hard for him to walk. Mitchell's mother started to stand up to give him her seat but Mitchell beat her to it!

"Here, take my seat, please," he said.

"Thank you," murmured the old man. He looked relieved to have a place to sit.

Mitchell stood beside his mother, holding tightly onto a pole. "For a four-year-old, you're pretty grown-up," she said to him with a warm smile.

If you are polite, you will think of offering your seat to someone who needs it more than you do.

It's polite to remember people's names.

Ryan's older brother Cameron was zipping up and down the street on his skateboard. Some of the younger children gathered on the sidewalk, to watch him spin and jump and do all kinds of tricks. Each time he sped by, he called out to one of them.

"Hi, Hannah! Hi, Ryan!"

When Janice waved to him he called over his shoulder. "Oh, hi Janice and brother Jason!" There didn't seem to be anything he couldn't do.

But to Joey he said, "And hi new kid whose name I can't remember." Poor Joey. Cameron remembered all their names except for his. And Joey had been having so much fun imagining what it would be like to have his own skateboard.

Next time Cameron went by, Joey took a deep breath and said, "My name's Joey."

"Oh, hi Joey," Cameron said with a laugh. "Want to try my skateboard when I'm finished?"

One of the best ways to make people feel they belong is to call them by name. If you don't know their name, ask them. They'll be glad you did.

Polite people wait their turn in line.

Tammy was excited because a special visitor named Carol had come to Kids' Klub. She had brought along baby chicks. Tammy had never seen chicks before. Everyone wanted to be the first to peer into the cage and to pick them up.

"You have to take turns," Carol explained. "Too many people at once will frighten the chicks."

They lined up patiently, except for Tammy. She began to push and shove the children in front of her. Pretty soon everyone was arguing.

"Oh-oh," Carol said, "you've scared the chicks. Now you'll have to wait for them to settle down before you can see them. It won't take long," she added cheerfully.

"But next time, please wait your turn. Then you will all get a chance to look at them and the chicks will feel happier too."

You wait in line so that everyone gets a turn, one at a time.

It's polite to send thank-you cards or letters.

A parcel wrapped in brown paper arrived in the mail for Colette one morning.

"Oh, I wonder who it's from!" she cried as she opened it. Inside she found a beautiful pink scarf. It was from her Aunt Clare because Colette had been trying her best and getting good marks at school.

"Why not write a note thanking her for thinking of you?" her mother suggested.

"Okay. I'll go sharpen my pencil crayons so I can draw a picture too."

But even though she had everything ready, Colette wasn't in the mood to write.

"I'll help you," her mother offered. "You'll see that it can really be fun."

They talked about what she could say in the letter. As they talked, Colette got all sorts of ideas.

Before she knew it, she had written her aunt a funny note with her favorite purple pencil crayon. It wasn't so hard to do after all. She even drew a funny picture of herself wearing the new scarf as a bandit's mask.

"I'll get an envelope for you and you can lick the stamp," her mother said.

"Who will mail it?" Colette asked.

"You will," her mother answered, "on our way to meet Dad at the bus stop."

It's always nice to get a card, letter or parcel in the mail. One of the best ways to say "thank you" is to write a note.

It's polite to accept a compliment without boasting.

It was a hot day. Ryan, Paul, Joey and Jason raced to the neighborhood pool as fast as they could.

Paul jumped right into the sparkling water.

"Boy, he's a good swimmer," Bobby said.

When Paul had joined his friends, Joey told him how good he was.

"Oh, I know," Paul said. "I'm good at lots of things."

"Oh, yeah?!" Bobby asked angrily. "How good are you at being shoved into the water?"

Just then, Paul's father came by and asked why they were fighting.

"Paul thinks he can do everything," Bobby muttered.

"He told me I was a good swimmer and I agreed with him and said I could do a lot of things well," Paul mumbled.

"It's best to say thank you at times like that," his father said. "No one likes people who boast."

It feels good to do something well. When others tell you that you're good at something, answer with a polite "thank you."

It's important to be polite to family members.

Ryan and his older brother Cameron were at home together after school one rainy afternoon.

"Here, hold this for me—just like this," Cameron ordered Ryan as he passed him the model airplane he'd been working on for days. "I want to paint the bottom of it, so don't move and don't put it down until I tell you to."

When he had finished helping Cameron, Ryan's mother came home, dripping wet. "Take my boots and umbrella down to the basement where they won't dirty anything," she said to Ryan. She didn't even say hello to him first. He felt like everybody was the boss, except him.

When his father came in later, Ryan was sitting in the living room, feeling bad.

"I'm home!" his father called out.

"I don't care. And whatever you've got I don't want to hold it, carry it or take it down to the basement!" Ryan muttered.

"What's the matter, Ryan?" his father asked as he walked over and sat down beside him.

"Everyone's telling me what to do all the time!" Ryan answered with a lump in his throat.

"Oh, I see," his father said, "and you just don't feel like taking orders anymore."

"That's right, I don't!" Ryan replied.

His father took his hand and stood up. "Okay, why don't you come with me and together we'll tell Cameron and Mom how you feel? Does that sound like a good idea?"

"Let's go!" Ryan said, holding onto his father's hand and smiling for the first time that afternoon.

It's easy for family members to take each other for granted. It's important to remember that *everyone* is happier to help if asked politely rather than told. Here are some easy ways to be polite:
- Use "please" and thank you."
- Wait in line without pushing or shoving.
- Try to make others feel comfortable and relaxed.
- Don't point or stare at other people.
- Say "excuse me" if you have to interrupt when others are talking.
- Send a thank-you note when somebody gives you a gift.

Printed and bound in U.S.A.